Creative Encounters:

A Collection of Encounter Lessons

by Barbara Fisher Mize

Illustrated by Bill Smith

Trillium Press
Monroe, New York

To Alan, a partner in a unique encounter of friendship

Copyright © 1988, Trillium Press, Inc.
All Rights Reserved.

Trillium Press, Inc.
PO Box 209
Monroe, NY 10950
(914) 783-2999

Trillium Press
203 College St., Suite 200
Toronto, Ontario
M5T 1P9 Canada

ISBN: 0-89824-248-7
Printed in the United States of America

TABLE OF CONTENTS

Introduction 1
English 3
Math 9
History 14
Science 20
Nature 28
Miscellaneous 36

Preface

In 1982 Creative Encounters appeared as a collection of encounter lessons for children in grades three and up. Its format was subject area groups of lessons; each lesson having a stated "scenario" and a series of focusing questions.

By 1985, English Language Arts and Reading Teachers discovered that the content and detail eliciting arrangement was easily adaptable to writing lessons whose aim was main idea development through supporting details. The fact that the lessons were grouped by subject area greatly facilitated writing activities to build interdisciplinary vocabulary. For the writing lesson, the "Scenario" became the theme/main idea. The lesson's expansion questions became supporting details. The encounter lesson became the class discussion, language experience, in preparation for writing. The writing activity was structured by the teacher according to the form being studied by the class: the descriptive paragraph, the narrative paragraph, the expository paragraph, poetry, a conversational piece, the friendly letter, the business letter, the essay, the very short story.

Other English Language Arts and Reading teachers have told us that *Creative Encounters* scenarios are excellent bases for imagery experiences. Using the techniques laid out by Bagley and Hess in *Two Hundred Ways of Using Imagery In the Classroom*, they have developed the stories as imagery lessons as a prelude to writing.

With this reprinting, Trillium Press thanks the English Language Arts and Reading Teachers who have ingeniously expanded the use of *Creative Encounters*.

Trillium Press, 1988

INTRODUCTION

The use of man's inner strengths and his perception of these strengths aids in the further development of his feelings about himself; this can be called self concept. If one values himself, believes himself to be capable, and generally expects to succeed in what he attempts, he is more free to venture into the unknown and challenge himself with new goals. Man achieves using his individual creative power as a result of using his individual strengths. An Encounter lesson will help the children in your classroom build their creative ability, self concept, and thought processes.

An encounter lesson is a lesson based on four principles which are expressed in terms of teacher behavior. The teacher will:

1. Help the student to think about who he is and what he can and ought to do.

2. Help the student to feel valuable and worthwhile.

3. Help the student to see learning as relevant to his individual needs.

4. Help the student to develop and maintain a learning atmosphere that reflects psychological safety and freedom.

Encounter lessons are short, lasting from twenty to thirty minutes. They are an "involving activity" in which the students, usually in small groups of 8 to 10, actively see, hear, taste, touch, smell and react to central stimuli. The objective is an "ENCOUNTER." It may take place with the stimulus, with ideas or with other people. The activities should be as open-ended as possible, thus giving each child an opportunity to bring his unique skills, abilities, and experiences to the task. In the encounter lesson the student is asked to become something else and to respond as though he were this new thing. He might become a page in a book, a geographical feature, or an apple pie. The students participating are then asked to respond to questions that fall into the following categories.

1. *Identitive*—who or what you are in your new role.

2. *Descriptive*—what you look like, other sensory information.

3. *Emotional*—how you feel about being this new thing.

4. *Creative*—how you change or add to yourself in this new role.

5. *Risk-taking or fearful*—the way you would react if presented with a threatening situation.

6. *Profound or abstract*—a message to someone or to the world from your new point of view.

Each time a question is asked, the leader starts with a different participant and each student responds in turn.

After the lesson, the leader talks with the participants about how they viewed their encounter and asks how they felt about being something else. The discussion turns to the "audience" and they give their reactions to the encounter group. The encounter lesson should be followed by "extenders;" activities of a wide variety that are related to the encounter lesson. These extenders encompass all subject matter areas. The encounter lesson has then stimulated interest in the area to be studied and has brought about a blend of cognitive and affective thinking.

FROM THE QUIETNESS OF THESE SHELVES

SCENARIO: Imagine yourselves in a very still place where there is only partial lighting and there are very crowded bookcases all around. You are a book in a library.

1. What kind of book are you?

2. It is night, and all of the books that weren't checked out are left on the shelves. How do you feel about not being checked out?

3. What do you talk about to the other books?

4. You are written in a different language than all the other books. How do you feel about this?

5. Someone is taking you off the shelf. He looks at you and then puts you back. How do you feel?

6. The librarian has set you back in the corner with some other books to be rebound. What would you say to the librarian if you could talk to her?

7. You are a book written in braille. How do you feel about that?

8. The library has decided to throw away some of its books. Explain why you think that you should not be discarded.

Kaye Vesely
Brevard County, Florida

ENGLISH   **3**

TO THE CITIZENS OF LILLIPUT

SCENARIO: You are a citizen of the famous town of Lilliput.

1. Where is your town, exactly?

2. How long have you lived here?

3. Do you hold any position in the town? What do you do?

4. What do you think of the king's palace? Would you like to live there? Why or why not?

5. What was your first thought when you saw Gulliver? Have you changed your first opinion of him? What made you change your mind?

6. Have you ever lived anywhere else?

7. What one thing would you like to tell the world from the point of view of short people?

8. If it were possible to change yourself in any way, would you consider it? How would you change yourself?

9. What do you see in the future?

STUART LITTLE

SCENARIO: You are like Stuart Little, the mouse born into the human family. You are two inches tall. A hawk is circling overhead but he hasn't seen you yet.

1. Where are you?

2. What are you wearing today?

3. How are you feeling?

4. What will you do to yourself so that the hawk will not see you?

5. All of a sudden the hawk sees a movement and dives in your direction. What will you do? Can you change yourself?

6. You have a message to send back to Mr. and Mrs. Little. What will you tell them?

Sheila Hawkins
Saskatoon Board of Education
Saskatoon, Saskatchewan
Canada

THE INVADER FROM PLANET X

SCENARIO: You are a space being from Planet X. You are just like Earth's human beings except that you have the ability to read any language.

1. Where would you go to learn about Planet Earth?

2. What could you learn about Planet Earth from the books in our school library?

3. Could you learn anything about Planet X?

4. You can't get a library card because you don't have a local address. How do you feel about this?

5. What stores would be most likely to be able to sell you information about our planet?

6. What kind of work could you do to earn the money?

Kaye Vesely
Brevard County, Florida

SCRABBLE

SCENARIO: You are the letter of your choice in a Scrabble set.

1. What letter are you and what is your point value?

2. You are part of a deluxe set; a luxury item that has been specially designed, signed by the artist, and numbered.
   a. What material are you made of?
   b. What typeface was used for lettering you?
   c. What does your board look like? Your box?

3. In the midst of the game, you suddenly feel yourself being knocked to the floor. You go unnoticed for the rest of the game. How do you feel?
4. What do you fear most while you are on the floor?

Phyllis Bray
Tampa, Florida

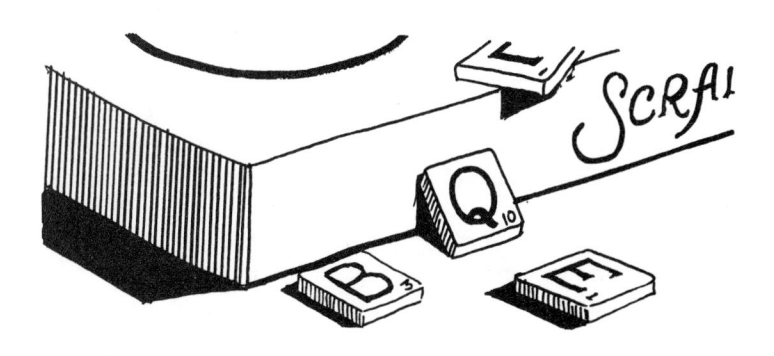

ENGLISH

POWERFUL ENDINGS

SCENARIO: You are to be a punctuation mark.

1. What punctuation mark are you?

2. Why do you feel that you are an important part of language or communication?

3. How does it feel to be misused? How do you feel when you are put in a place where you do not belong?

4. Who do you like to be used by most? (Children, a great writer, a song writer, etc.).

5. How do you feel when you are completely left out of where you belong?

6. If you could change yourself, or perhaps your appearance, what would you want to be instead of what you are? Why?

7. What advice do you have to give to a beginning class in English? Why do you feel that you are qualified to give such advice?

8. What sort of relationships do you have with the other forms of punctuation? Are you all in one family?

9. Do you speak the same language as all forms of punctuation?

8   ENGLISH

NUMBERS

SCENARIO: Imagine yourself to be a number. Take on the shape and the value of that number.

1. What number are you?

2. Are you a reversible number like a 6 or a 9? How do you feel about your shape?

3. Would you rather be added or subtracted? Multiplied or divided?

4. Do you enjoy being by yourself or in a group?

5. Have you ever been on a calendar?

6. If you could be anywhere and be used anywhere, where would it be? What would your function be?

7. What is your dream for the future?

8. Can you be more than one place at a time? How? Have you ever done this?

MATH 9

ALONG THE STRAIGHT AND NARROW

SCENARIO: Imagine yourself to be a line.

1. What color are you?

2. Where are you?

3. What is your greatest talent?

4. Do you feel it is better to be a straight narrow line or a curved fat one?

5. How are you misused?

6. How do you feel about the dot?

7. What is your favorite subject in school?

8. Is there any event in history that might not have happened without you?

9. Do you have any specific job?

10. If you could be used in creating something, what would it be? Who would use you?

DOT

SCENARIO: Imagine yourself to be a dot.

1. Where are you?
2. Do you travel around? Where do you go? How do you move?
3. Where is your favorite place?
4. How do you feel about the line?
5. Could you be a dot without the line?
6. Are you a whole dot? A hollow dot? An invisible dot?
7. What has been your greatest task?
8. Are you ever confused with a period?
9. If you could talk, what advice would you give someone who might use you?

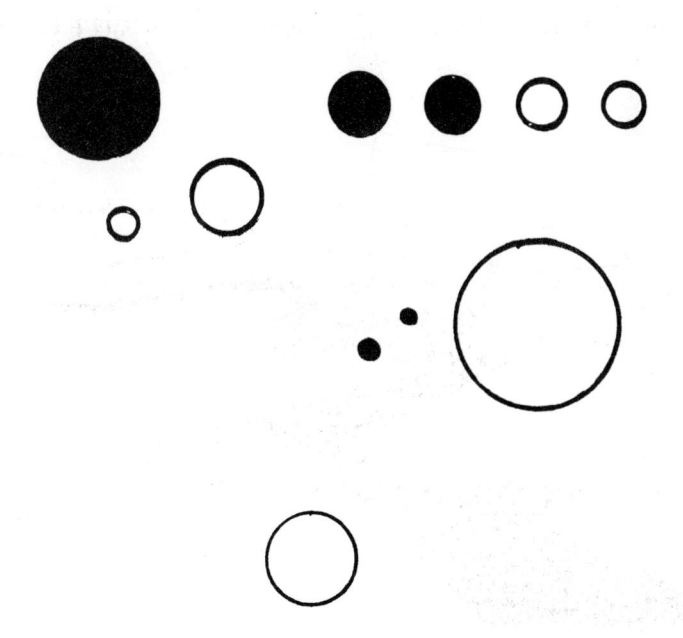

MATH 11

HEY, ALL YOU SQUARES

SCENARIO: Five of you are squares, and one of you is a triangle.

1. Squares, how do you feel about the triangle?

2. Would you consider letting the triangle into your group?

3. What kind of shape would you consider letting into your group?

4. Triangle, how do you feel about the situation?

5. What group do you feel you could fit into besides just another triangle group?

6. Triangle, what could you do to make better use of yourself while in the middle of all these squares?

7. The world is now a system of only circles. How do all of you feel about this?

DIRECTIONS

SCENARIO: You are a compass.

1. Have you ever lost your sense of direction?

2. Did any great explorers ever use you? Who?

3. Have you ever felt useless? When?

4. Is there any way you can be wrong?

5. Have you ever been wrong? What happened?

6. When have you been the most proud of yourself?

7. Do you think that there could possibly be any way to improve compasses so that they may be better?

MATH   13

HOW

SCENARIO: You are the turquoise stones in an Indian chief's necklace. The chief lives on a reservation in the West.

1. Where did you originate?

2. How were you mined?

3. What is your life like on a reservation?

4. Has life for the Indians changed? How?

5. What changes have you seen in the countryside?

6. Were you a medium of exchange?

7. Is there any folklore regarding your history?

8. If you could change one thing for the Indians, what would that be?

9. What do you predict will happen to the Indian culture?

10. Why do you suppose you're so popular today?

Sue Cameron
Brevard County Schools, Florida

THE CROWN JEWELS

SCENARIO: You are the jewels on Henry VIII's crown and you have just been brought to a famous museum.

1. In which museum would you like to be? Why?

2. What other masterpieces would you like to surround you in the museum?

3. What are the other masterpieces telling you?

4. How are people of today who pass you the same or different from people in Henry VIII's time?

5. What are people saying about you? How do you feel when people walk right by and ignore you?

6. Can you change your appearance?

7. After living with each other for hundreds of years, how would you feel if someone substituted a fake stone for one of the gems in the crown?

8. What do you talk about when the museum closes to the public?

9. If you could be used to crown any person today, who would it be? Why?

Sue Cameron
Brevard County Schools

YELLOW FEVER

SCENARIO: It is a humid night and you have just paused to rest on a leaf. You are a mosquito carrying the yellow fever epidemic.

1. Where have you been?

2. Where do you live?

3. Are you aware that you are spreading a disease? How do you feel about this?

4. How do you avoid being killed?

5. How do you feel since everyone is trying to kill you?

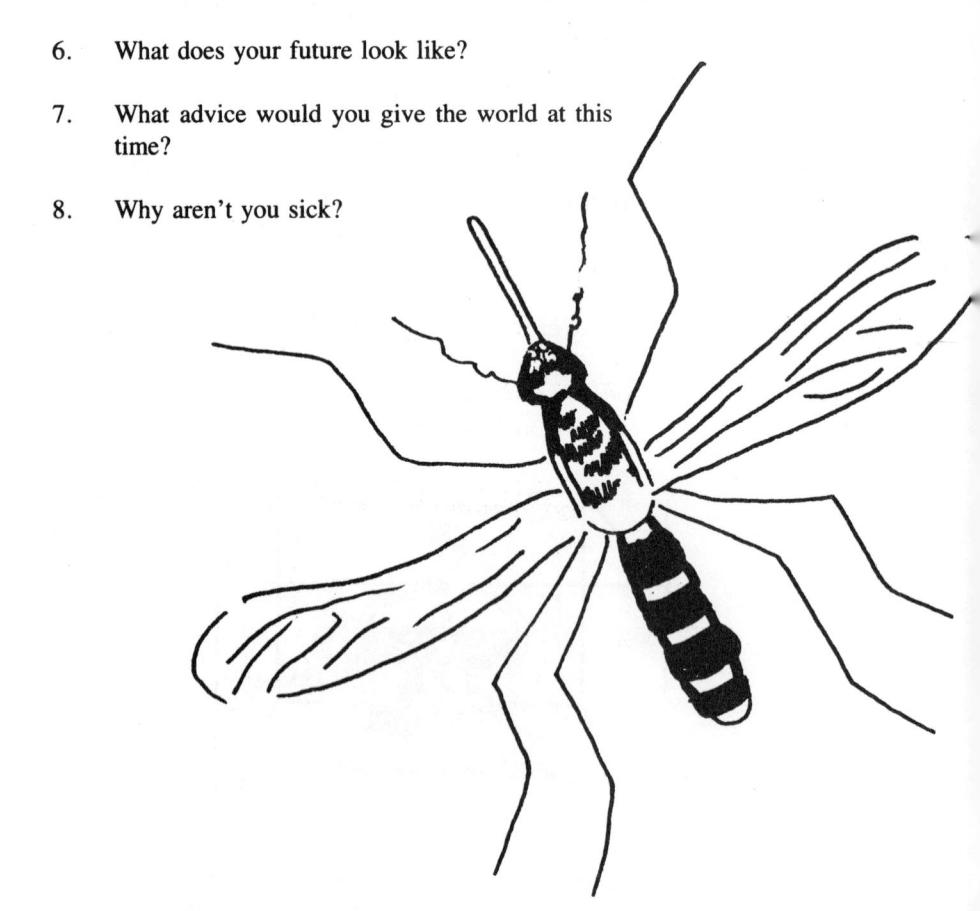

6. What does your future look like?

7. What advice would you give the world at this time?

8. Why aren't you sick?

IN THE CONGRESS

SCENARIO: Your arms and legs are getting heavier and much harder—you are becoming more stiff and rigid—you are becoming a chair which is located in Congress in Washington, D.C.

1. How long have you been in Congress?

2. Who is the most famous person to use you?

3. What is the most important event you have witnessed?

4. How would you change yourself to make yourself more useful or attractive?

5. If you could deliver a speech, what would you discuss?

6. Who has been your favorite president? Why?

7. If you could move anywhere, where would you go?

GOVERNMENTAL COMPUTERS

SCENARIO: You are a computer being used by a governmental agency is Washington, D.C.

1. What agency or office are you in?

2. What color are you, how big are you and what do you look like?

3. How do you like helping this agency?

4. If you could do something different for this agency, what would you do?

5. A class of 6th graders is touring your office and they are walking toward you. What are you thinking?

6. If you could tell the people who work with you something about the work that their agency does, what would you tell them?

18 HISTORY

ARCHEOLOGY

SCENARIO: You are an artifact from the Tomb of King Tut.

1. What are you made of?

2. Where in the tomb were you found?

3. What was your opinion of the King?

4. What would your reaction have been if the tomb was invaded by robbers?

5. What can you tell us about the curse of King Tut?

6. Now that you are no longer in the tomb, what are your plans for the future?

7. How do you feel about being in a museum and on public view?

Wendy Cutts
Orlando, Florida

HISTORY **19**

A SCIENTIFIC TUBE

SCENARIO: Imagine yourself to be on a steel table in a laboratory. You are a test tube.

1. What are you made of?

2. Whose laboratory are you in?

3. What are you being used for now?

4. Do those chemicals tickle? What do they feel like?

5. What do you hold?

6. Do you like being long and thin?

7. Were you ever anything else besides a test tube?

8. What is the greatest experiment that you have ever been a part of?

9. How do you feel about Bunsen burners?

10. Would you like to be anything else?

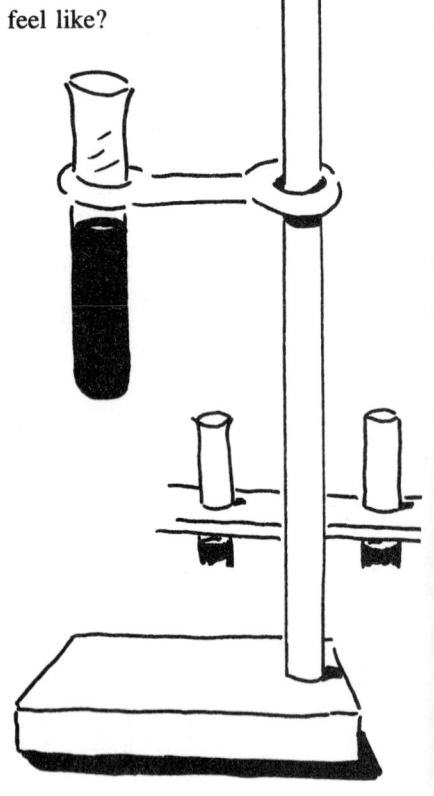

A FOSSIL

SCENARIO: Feel yourself growing older and harder—you are becoming a fossil.

1. What type of fossil are you?

2. If someone were to find you, what would you look like? How would you feel to your discoverer?

3. What is the best thing that has happened to you as a fossil?

4. If you were to dissolve, what type of new animal or plant would you like to come back as?

5. How would you feel if an archeologist were digging in your area?

6. If you could talk, what bit of wisdom could you pass on?

Lisa Craig
Debby Holsonback
Tampa, Florida

SWIMMING IN THE TRIANGLE

SCENARIO: Imagine that you are a fish in the Bermuda Triangle.

1. What is your biggest secret?

2. What does the Bermuda Triangle look like?

3. Have you been here long? How did you get here? Why do you think it is such a mystery?

4. Have you ever seen any of the missing ships or planes?

5. What are the storms like here?

6. Do you know what happened to the people on the ships?

7. How do you feel about living here? Does it scare you at all? Why or why not?

8. Would you rather live somewhere else?

9. Why haven't you disappeared?

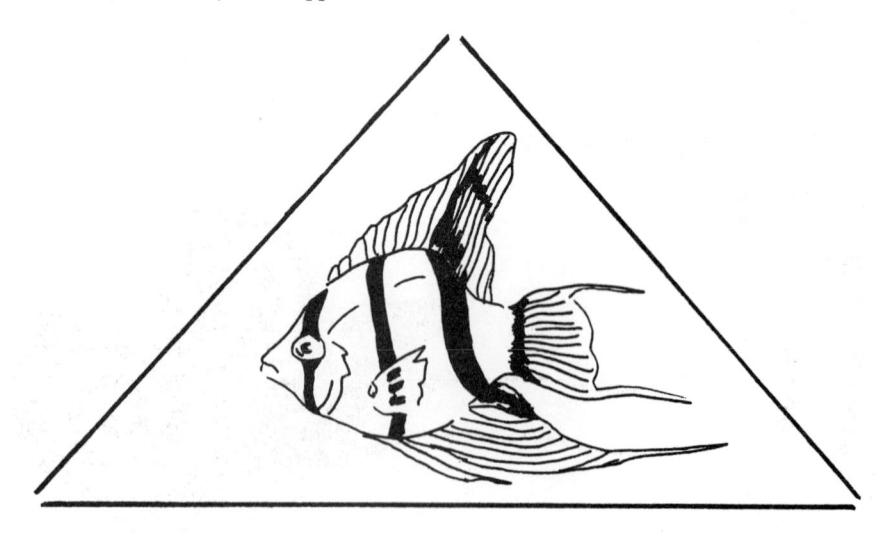

STIRRUPS, ANVILS AND SUCH

SCENARIO: There are many parts of an ear, but imagine that you are a bone in the ear.

1. What bone are you?

2. What is your environment like? What does it feel like?

3. Do you have any neighbors? How do you feel about them?

4. What do you think is your most important function?

5. If you could be moved to another part of the body, where would you go, and why? How would this move affect the ear?

6. Are you totally independent?

7. If you could function in the outside world, at what job would you be best?

8. Can you hear, see, feel?

9. What has been the most traumatic thing that has ever happened to you?

10. If you had one chance to speak at an American Medical Association meeting, what would be your main topic?

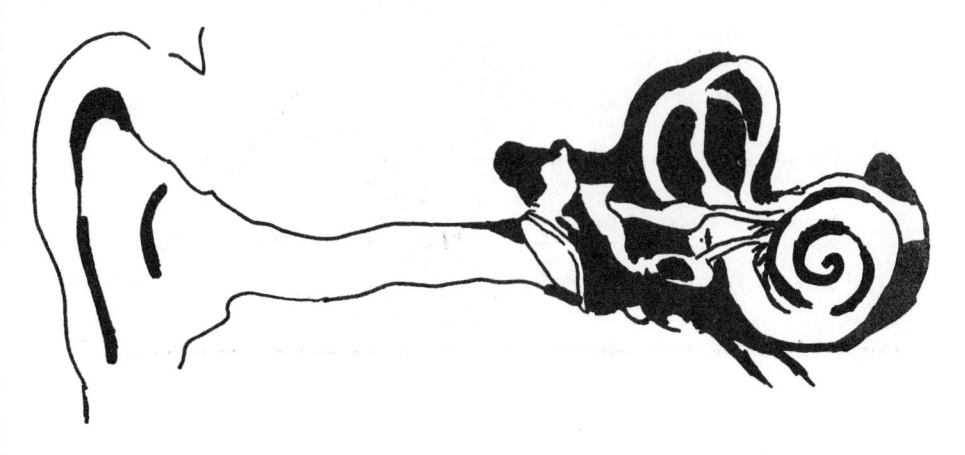

SCIENCE

INNER WORKS

SCENARIO: You are a muscle in the human body.

1. Where do you live?

2. What do you do?

3. Have you ever been sick? What effect did that have?

4. Does the weather affect you at all?

5. Have you always been in this body or are you a transplant?

6. How do you feel about transplants?

7. Have you ever been involved in an operation? What was it like?

8. Whose body are you in now?

9. What is your relationship with the brain?

10. Do you have blood vessels running through you? How does this feel?

11. Have you ever felt like just "closing up shop" and taking a vacation? What would happen if you did? Where would you go? What preparations would you have to make to get ready?

12. Do you feel useful? Why or why not?

13. What does it take to make you happy?

14. What makes you sad?

15. What advice would you like to give to humans?

DEATH AND DYING

SCENARIO: Your doctor has told you that you have a terminal illness.

1. What type of illness do you have?

2. How long will you live?

3. How do you feel today?

4. During your projected amount of time remaining, what would you really like to do?

5. The doctor has just told you that through extensive treatment, you may live a bit longer. He cannot say how long exactly. How do you feel? Will you take the treatment? The choice is entirely up to you.

6. During your illness you have been in and out of the hospital for 6 months. Upon returning this time, you learn that there is a new teenage patient in for treatment for an illness similar to yours. The doctor asks you to talk to this person. What would you like to say?

7. During your illness, have your feelings changed toward your parents, doctor, siblings, etc.?

8. Have you discussed funeral preparations with your family? What are they?

9. What message would you like to leave with the living?

10. What would you like your grieving loved ones to say about you?

Jane Gradewell
Montgomery County, Penn.

NEWLY PLANTED

SCENARIO: Imagine yourself as a newly planted seed deep in the dark, cool ground.

1. What kind of seed are you?

2. Who planted you and why?

3. What would you like your purpose in life to be?

4. Bugs are chewing at your roots. How do you feel about this?

5. It is night time. Tomorrow you will have grown enough to break through the ground. As you anticipate this, how do you think you will react?

6. You made it to the surface! How does it feel?

7. How do you feel on stormy days? On sunny days?

Connie McInnis
Hillsborough County, Florida

UP ABOVE THE WORLD SO HIGH

SCENARIO: Imagine that you are high in the sky and that you feel very warm. You are a star.

1. Where are you now? Have you ever seen the Earth?

2. How do you feel about what you do and where you are?

3. Do you have other friends? Where are they?

4. How do you feel about the USA's space program?

5. Has the invention of the telescope affected you any?

6. What do you consider to be your ultimate contribution to space?

7. Have you ever been "wished upon"? What does it feel like?

8. Do you expect ever to fall from space? What are your feelings about this? Where would you like to land? Why?

9. Do you feel as though you are alone?

10. Do other stars talk to you? Do you ever feel like you are being watched?

11. What do you do when the moon does not come out? Do you work to shine brighter? What makes you twinkle?

12. Where do you go and what do you do in the daytime?

13. How is "stardust" made?

14. What do you look like? Do you really have five points? Six points? Are you a color, or are you clear?

15. Do you stay in one place or do you move around?

SCIENCE

SEVERAL ENCOUNTERS OF TREES

SCENARIO: You are a tree in the forest. The trees are being cut down to go to a mill to be made into paper.

1. What kind of tree are you?

2. How old are you?

3. What memories of the forest do you have?

4. How do you think it will feel to be cut down?

5. Do you want to be made into paper?

TREES CONTINUED

SCENARIO: There was a forest fire in a section of the forest about a year ago. There are still many burnt stumps and charred remains of the disaster, which keeps it in the minds of all. You are a tiny seedling just beginning to grow in the darkened ground.

1. Do you wonder why the ground is so black and bare?

2. Are there strange smells which you cannot quite understand?

3. How did you get here?

4. Do you know what caused the fire?

5. How does it feel to be a tiny tree in such a dark and desolate place?

SCENARIO: Winter has come to the forest. Your leaves have long since fallen. You are covered with a layer of snow.

1. How did you feel when your leaves fell off?

2. How does the snow feel on your branches?

3. Are you anxious for winter to end?

4. How do you feel about the coming of spring?

5. What has happened to your friends now that winter has come?
Mary Schlachter
Levy County, Florida

SPRING BUTTERFLIES

SCENARIO: It is a beautiful day in April, and you are a butterfly that has just landed on a flower.

1. What type of butterfly are you? Describe yourself.

2. How old are you?

3. Have you spent any time in a cocoon? If so, where was it? How long did it take you to build it? (or did you have it made?) What did it feel like in the cocoon? What was yours made of?

4. What type of flower are you on?

5. Why did you land on this flower?

6. Where are you and the flower? In some king's garden perhaps, or just outside somewhere?

7. What are you thinking about right now?

8. What are your plans for the future?

9. Do you have any message to give the world?

SMALL WORKERS

SCENARIO: Ants are social insects and always live in groups. They live in communities much like our human communities. In each community every ant has a job to do. You are an ant.

1. How old are you?

2. What is your job?

3. What are some of the requirements of your job?

4. What do you like to do when you are not busy with your specialty?

5. Who or what is your worst enemy?

6. What do you do when it rains?

7. Who is your favorite ant? Why?

8. What would you do if an anteater invaded your ant hill and began eating his lunch?

9. What do you feel is your best form of defense?

10. How do you communicate with other ants? Can you talk to other animals?

11. What does it feel like to be sitting out in the grass?

12. Are you affected by the seasons?

13. How do you feel about insecticides?

MUSHROOMS

SCENARIO: There are hundreds of varieties of mushrooms commonly found in the woods during the "mushroom months" of August and September. You are a mushroom and it is an early day in August just after a rain.

1. How do you feel right now? Are you wet? Why or why not?

2. What were you doing just before the rain?

3. What kind of mushroom are you? What color are you? Are you safe to eat?

4. Where do you get your food? What do you like to eat?

5. What is the most exciting thing you have ever done?

6. What do you hope to do tomorrow?

7. What do you think will happen to you by November?

A PART

SCENARIO: You are part of a rain forest.

1. What are you?

2. How did you get where you are now?

3. How long have you been part of this forest?

4. Who or what is your best friend here? Why?

5. How do you feel about animals in the forest?

6. Would if affect you any if man decided to camp, hunt, and fish in your forest? Why?

7. What is the most helpful thing you have ever done?

8. Do you have any enemies? Do you have any defense or protection against them?

9. Are you affected at all by the weather? How? What type of weather is your favorite?

10. How would you feel if you were moved to the desert? How would it affect how you survived?

SOARING

SCENARIO: You are a bird.

1. What type of bird are you?

2. Where do you live? Do you live alone?

3. What do you look like?

4. What is your favorite food? How do you get your food?

5. Are you a daytime or a nighttime bird?

6. How high can you fly? Have you ever flown above the clouds? What does it feel like to fly through a cloud? What is it like above the clouds? Can you land on a cloud? Have you ever tried that? What happened? What was it like?

7. Where is your nest?

8. Do you migrate? When and where do you go? How long does it take to get there?

9. Do you ever get bored just flying around and sitting in trees?

10. What do you do for excitement?

BEACHED

SCENARIO: You are something on a section of beach on the West Coast of Africa.

1. What are you?

2. How did you get there?

3. Many African children play on your beach. Describe your own experience in one of their games.

4. You overhear one of the children call his brothers and sisters home because a huge hurricane is approaching You are left alone. What runs through your mind?

5. If you were to send the children of the world a message to make them realize your potential for games, what would you say?

Cindy Nevins
University of South Florida
Tampa, Florida

SMALL FRIENDS IN THE FOREST

SCENARIO: Begin to think of yourself as growing smaller—smaller and even smaller—you are now a gnome in a forest.

1. How old are you?

2. Why do you live so long?

3. Where do you live? What is your house made of?

4. What is your job? Do you prefer to be inside or outside during the day? Why?

5. What is your favorite thing to do? Do you do anything special for holidays? Which ones? What do you do?

6. Do you have any enemies? How do you protect yourself against them?

7. What do you eat? Why?

8. What do you do when it rains or snows?

9. How do you travel?

10. What is the most helpful deed that you have ever done?

11. Have you ever done anything bad?

12. You have lived for some time. Do you have any advice to share?

MISCELLANEOUS

ONCE UPON A BENCH

SCENARIO: It is a very nice spring day and people are bustling by you—you are a bench.

1. What type of bench are you?

2. What are you made of?

3. Are you an old or a new bench?

4. Where are you?

5. Who sits on you most of the time?

6. Who would you most like to use you?

7. The movers are coming tomorrow. Where do you hope they will take you?

8. Do you look forward to leaving this place? Why or why not?

9. What is your favorite pastime?

10. What has been your most exciting experience?

11. How do you feel you could benefit society?

12. If you could have a sign painted on you, what would it say?

MISCELLANEOUS

STICK 'EM UP

SCENARIO: You are some unset precious gems in a jewelry store. Some armed, masked men have just entered the store.

1. Why do you suppose the masked men are here?

2. Do the masked men want you? Why or why not? How do you feel about that?

3. Do the guns scare you? Why? Why not?

4. Will you miss the other jewels in the store? Why? Why not?

5. What would you like to be made into?

6. What is going to become of you if you are stolen?

7. How can you help the authorities find you?

8. Why do you think people break the law?

9. Why are laws important?

Sue Cameron
Brevard County Schools, Florida

NEW ARRIVAL ON THE COLOR WHEEL

SCENARIO: You are the first new color to be discovered in thousands of years.

1. What color are you?

2. What do you look like? Are you like any other color we know?

3. How do you feel about being discovered and why did you wait so long?

4. If you could mix with another color to become something different, what color would you mix with? If you could take the place (or role) of another color, whose place would you take? (for instance, taking the place of yellow for the sun)

5. If the World Color Organization was going to place you between two colors, which two would they be? If they were to challenge your right to be added to our list of other colors, what would you tell them? Why are you valuable?

6. What does your color say? How should we feel when we see you?

Stephanie Riess
Pinellas County Schools, Florida

FILMMAKING

SCENARIO: Pretend you are a camera.

1. What kind of camera would you like to be? What name would you give yourself?

2. What would you like to see?

3. What do you think when people make you see things you do not want to see? What do you think when you see those things you like?

4. What improvements would you like to make on yourself?

5. A child wants to see how you work. What are your feelings about this?

6. Which of your many experiences would you like to share with your colleagues or with the world?

Roger Stahl
Florida

ROLLING ALONG

SCENARIO: Imagine yourself to be a ball.

1. What are you made of and what do you look like?

2. How do you feel about being a ball?

3. If you could change yourself, what would you become and why?

4. If you were used for soccer how would you feel?

5. If you could use yourself as a means of communication, what would you tell others?

Elizabeth Wolfe
University of South Florida
Tampa, Florida

IN THE CLOSET

SCENARIO: You are a game in your closet at home.

1. What kind of game are you?

2. Where did you come from? To whom do you belong?

3. What kind of condition are you in now?

4. Who plays with you?

5. What was the worst thing that ever happened to you?

6. What kind of affect do you have on people?

   How would you feel if you were lost?

8. Do you ever travel?

9. How old are you?

10. Would you like to change and if so, how?

Cheryl Winegar
Tampa, Florida

WITH STRINGS

SCENARIO: Pretend you are a marionette in a traveling puppet show.

1. What character are you?

2. Describe yourself. What characters do you play in the puppet show? What are you wearing?

3. The puppeteer has decided to star you in his new show. How do you feel about being the center of attention?

4. One child cried when you were performing. How did you feel about that? Did you worry that you were causing the crying?

5. You have always wanted to star in a new show. What story would you like to do? Who would you like to be?

6. The puppeteer has tangled your strings, and you are afraid you will fall or bump into another marionette. What would you do?

7. If you could talk to the audience from your own heart, what would you like to say?

Susan Fernandez
Hillsborough County, Florida

MISCELLANEOUS

SETTING THE STAGE

SCENARIO: You are a newly designed lighting instrument, a revolution in the area of stage lighting.

1. What do you look like?

2. What sets you apart from the fresnel and the lecko and other lighting instruments?

3. What is your best quality?

4. If you came with directions, what would they say?

5. Where would you most like to be used?

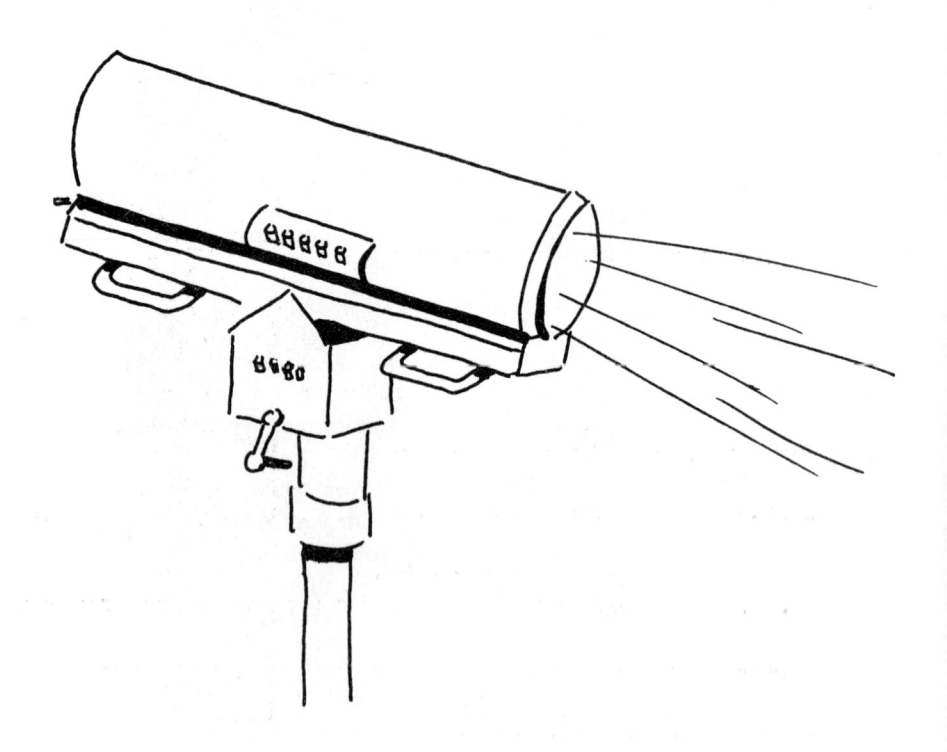

MISCELLANEOUS

SCENIC THOUGHTS

SCENARIO: You are a piece of scenery; a flat used in a very famous play.

1. In what play are you?

2. Are you an interior or an exterior flat? Describe yourself in detail.

3. If you could talk to your designer, what would you say?

4. You have been used for a long time, and now you are going to be whitewashed and redone. How do you feel about this?

5. If you could tell the world about your job and your experiences, what would you say?

RACY THOUGHTS

SCENARIO: You are a race car in the Daytona 500.

1. Who is driving you?

2. What is the weather like?

3. Is this a good day for you?

4. Do you anticipate any problems?

5. What do you feel you have to do to win?

6. How will you feel if you lose?

7. What do you think about as you are going through your laps?

Judy Kasweck
Brevard County, Florida

THE FAMILY CAR

SCENARIO: You are a station wagon for a family of six.

1. Where do you live?

2. What is your favorite errand? Do you enjoy family vacations?

3. One of the children has just dropped an ice cream cone on your seat. How do you feel?

4. Where do you go at night?

5. If you could alter one thing about your owner and family, what would you change?

6. You are the carrier of the Little League team. How do you react to carrying some of the team and all of their equipment?

7. What is your favorite treat?

Judy Kasweck
Brevard County, Florida

A MAGIC WAND

SCENARIO: Imagine yourself to be a magic wand. You may be any shape you wish. Think a moment about exactly how you look and then begin to reflect about some of your experiences.

1. What are you made of?

2. How big are you?

3. What exactly do you look like?

4. To whom do you belong? Have you had other owners?

5. What makes you work? Do you ever get tired or break down?

6. What is the best thing you have ever done?

7. What is the worst thing you have ever done? Why did you do it?

8. How would you convince someone to believe in magic?

9. Do you think that everyone should have a magic wand? Why or why not?

10. What is your philosophy about the use of magic?

MISCELLANEOUS

TAXI! TAXI!

SCENARIO: You are a taxi cab in a very large city.

1. Where are you?

2. What do you look like?

3. Where do you go most frequently?

4. What is the most exciting thing that has ever happened to you?

5. What is going to happen to you when you grow old and see yourself being replaced by a shiny, new, energetic model?

6. What is the most beautiful sight you have ever seen?

7. Do you feel you are an integral part of American life? Why or why not?
        Judy Kasweck
        Brevard County, Florida

THE LOST BALL

SCENARIO: You are a small rubber ball that has just been found after being buried in the sand.

1. How long have you been there?

2. Who lost you? Who found you?

3. What were you doing when you were lost?

4. How was it that you were discovered?

5. Now that you are out in society, for what would you like to be used? Do you think you would have any use in math circles?

6. What is your name and what color are you?

Denis Fredrick
Washington

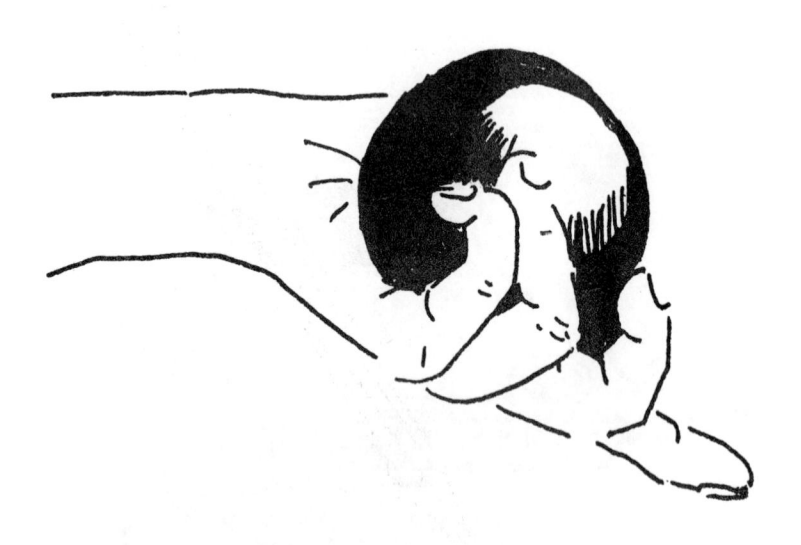

PENCIL PUSHER

SCENARIO: You are a pencil.

1. Describe yourself to us.

2. You are only used to draw squares. How do you feel about that? Would you like to draw other things? What things?

3. How do you feel about going into the sharpener?

4. Your last inch of lead has just broken. What is your fondest memory?

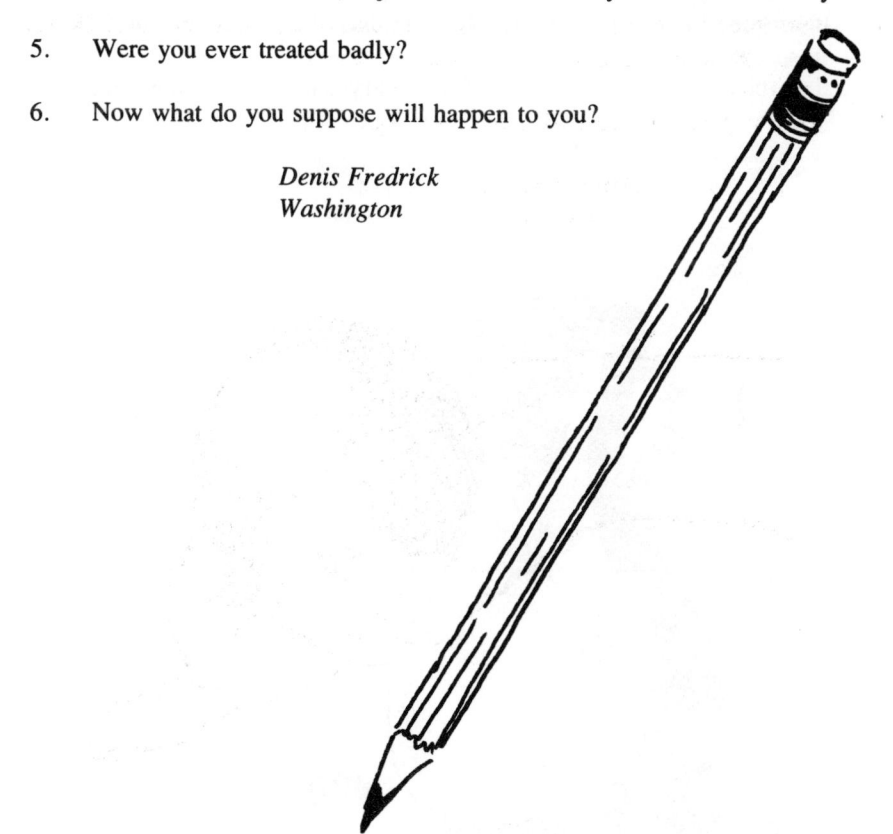

5. Were you ever treated badly?

6. Now what do you suppose will happen to you?

Denis Fredrick
Washington

POTTERY

SCENARIO: Imagine that you are a shard of old pottery that has just been dug up by someone.

1. What color are you? Is your surface smooth or rough?

2. Are you happy with what you are? How could you improve yourself?

3. If your owner were to change you in some way how would you want to be changed?

4. If someone dropped you in a bucket of red paint, what would you think or feel?

5. If you could talk for five minutes, what would you tell people about yourself?

Susie Gearen
Gaye Gregory
Hillsborough County, Florida

TO BE FOUND IN FRANCE

SCENARIO: You are a famous object in the capital of France. You can be a structure, a building, a statue, etc.

1. What are you?

2. Why do you like or dislike being what you are?

3. How do you feel about having thousands of tourists around you all of the time?

4. What color would you like to be painted? Why?

5. If you could say something to all of those people who look at you, walk on you or go around touching you, what would you say?

Dawana Edwards
University of South Florida
Tampa, Florida

MISCELLANEOUS

SPANISH WORDS

SCENARIO: You are a Spanish word.

1. Which word are you?

2. What kind of sound does your word make?

3. What kind of feeling do you get when people say you?

4. How would you make more than one of you?

5. If you were on a sign and a man were to take your letters down, would this destroy you?

6. Suppose you suddenly became known as a bad word. Would that make you feel bad inside?

Judith Nusen
Horizon School
Tampa, Florida

CHINESE FOOTSTEPS

SCENARIO: You are a "geta", a Chinese type of sandal.

1. What materials are you made of?

2. To whom do you belong?

3. What sort of sensations do you feel when you meet all the other "getas" inside the door of your family's house? Why are you all just inside the door?

4. If you could change your appearance, what would you do?

5. You are going out in a monsoon. What kind of feelings are you experiencing?

6. How will you feel when your owner decides to buy a new pair of "geta"?

Hilda Rosselli
Hillsborough County, Florida

COOKING

SCENARIO: Imagine you are a baking dish in a cupboard and it is late at night.

1. What do you look like?

2. Are you a large or small dish?

3. Are you happy being what you are?

4. If you could add or take away something about yourself, how would you change?

5. If you could talk to your owner, what would you say you wanted baked in you? What other advice might you give?

Nancy Towne
Tampa, Florida